Part 1: Learning The Alphabet

a b c d e f g h i j k l m n o p q r s t u v w x y z

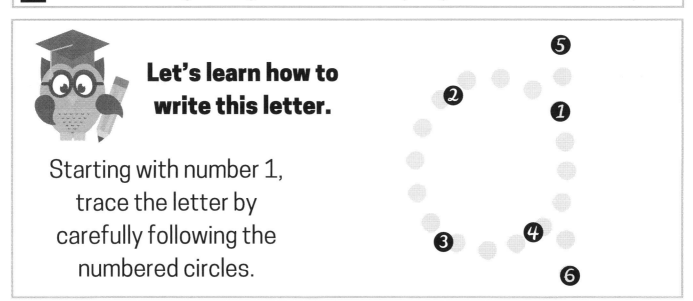

Let's learn how to write this letter.

Starting with number 1, trace the letter by carefully following the numbered circles.

Now let's practice! Trace the letters using the example above.

a a a a a a a a a a a a a

a a a a a a a a a a a a a

a a a a a a a a a a a a a

Your turn! Write the letter on your own.

a

HANDWRITING WORKBOOK FOR KIDS

Welcome to Brighter Child's *Handwriting Workbook For Kids*. This workbook has been specifically designed to take your child from the very beginning of their writing journey to the stage where they are confidently writing words and sentences.

The workbook uses Brighter Child's unique 'dot to dot' illustrated exercise system so kids can easily trace the letters and learn the correct sequence in which to perform their pencil strokes. This ensures they form the correct writing habits from the earliest stage to write well-formed letters and words.

HOW THIS WORKBOOK IS STRUCTURED

This workbook is split into the following parts.

Part 1: The Alphabet

Learn to write every letter of the alphabet - uppercase and lowercase - until each one has been perfected. Use the dot to dot method for easy learning.

Part 2: Writing Words

Now we use all the skills we have learnt so far to write a selection of words. We start easy and work up to more complex words.

Part 3: Writing Sentences

The final stage builds on all the practice in parts 1 and 2 to allow the child to write complete sentences.

Brighter Child Company

AVAILABLE ON AMAZON

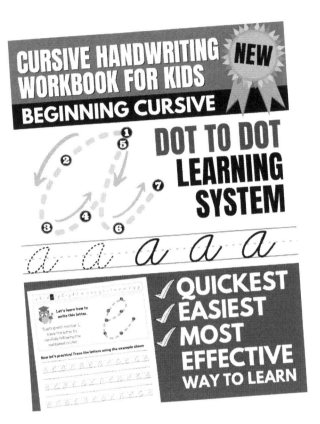

CURSIVE HANDWRITING WORKBOOK FOR KIDS
NEW
BEGINNING CURSIVE

DOT TO DOT LEARNING SYSTEM

✔ QUICKEST
✔ EASIEST
✔ MOST EFFECTIVE
WAY TO LEARN

THE IDEAL STARTING WORKBOOK FOR LEARNING CURSIVE HANDWRITING

- 8.5" x 11" - Large size pages
- Learn to write the cursive alphabet easily
- Unique 'dot-to-dot' system
- Perfect for grades 2-5
- Over 100 pages

UNIQUE VISUAL METHOD MAKES LEARNING NUMERACY EASY AND FUN

- Part 1: Master writing each number
- Part 2: Introduction to addition
- Part 3: Addition exercises
- Part 4: Introduction to subtraction
- Part 5: Subtraction exercises

MATH K
KINDERGARTEN WORKBOOK
ADDITION & SUBTRACTION

VISUAL LEARNING SYSTEM

$1 + 2 = \square$

$10 - \square = 7$

LOTS OF DOTS - PART 2

✔ QUICKEST
✔ EASIEST
✔ MOST EFFECTIVE
WAY TO LEARN

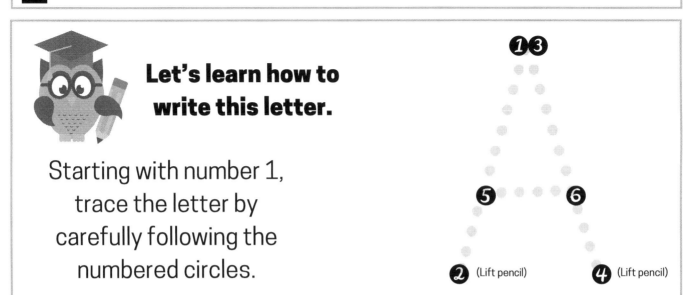

Let's learn how to write this letter.

Starting with number 1, trace the letter by carefully following the numbered circles.

❶❸

❺ **❻**

❷ (Lift pencil)   **❹** (Lift pencil)

Now let's practice! Trace the letters using the example above.

Your turn! Write the letter on your own.

A

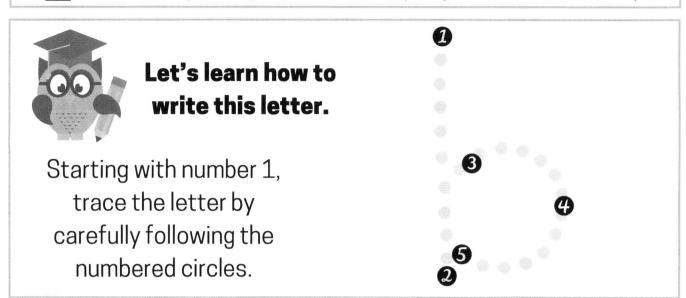

Let's learn how to write this letter.

Starting with number 1, trace the letter by carefully following the numbered circles.

Now let's practice! Trace the letters using the example above.

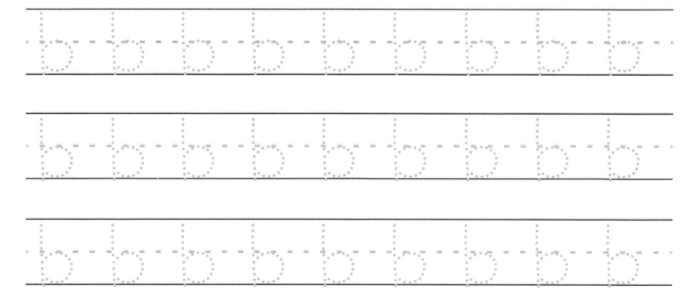

Your turn! Write the letter on your own.

b

A B C D E F G H I J K L M N O P Q R S T U V W X Y Z

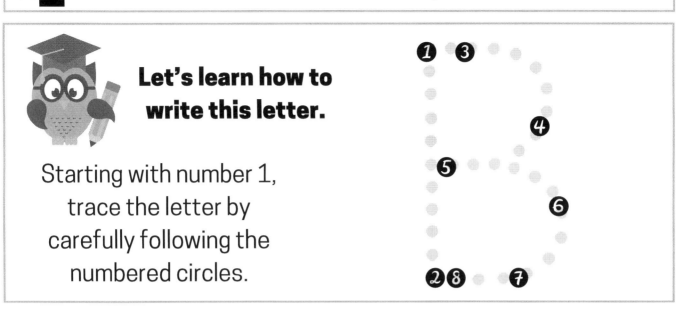

Let's learn how to write this letter.

Starting with number 1, trace the letter by carefully following the numbered circles.

Now let's practice! Trace the letters using the example above.

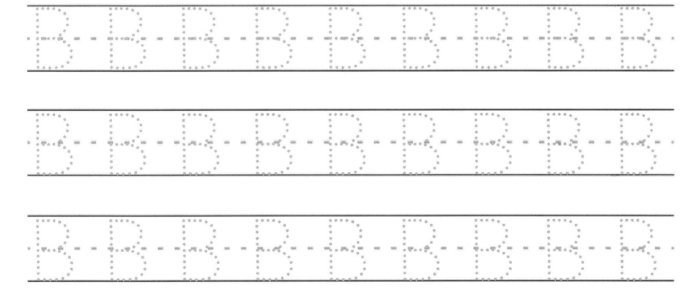

Your turn! Write the letter on your own.

B

a b **c** d e f g h i j k l m n o p q r s t u v w x y z

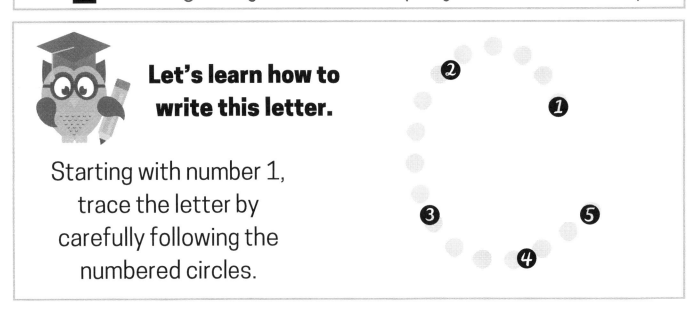

Let's learn how to write this letter.

Starting with number 1, trace the letter by carefully following the numbered circles.

Now let's practice! Trace the letters using the example above.

c c c c c c c c c c c c c c

c c c c c c c c c c c c c c

c c c c c c c c c c c c c c

Your turn! Write the letter on your own.

C

A B **C** D E F G H I J K L M N O P Q R S T U V W X Y Z

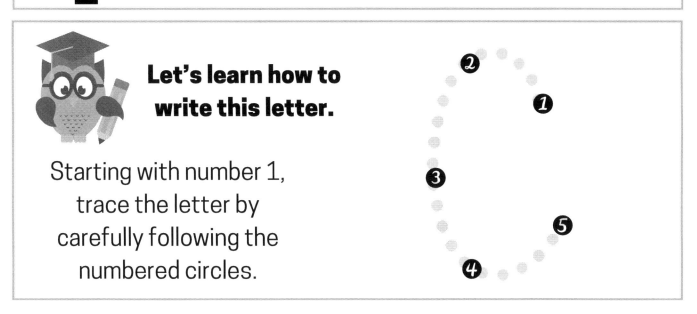

Let's learn how to write this letter.

Starting with number 1, trace the letter by carefully following the numbered circles.

Now let's practice! Trace the letters using the example above.

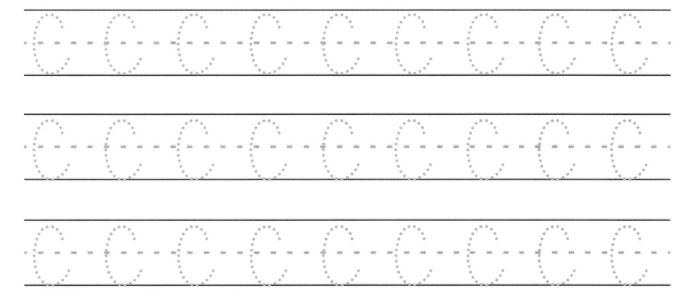

Your turn! Write the letter on your own.

C

a b c **d** e f g h i j k l m n o p q r s t u v w x y z

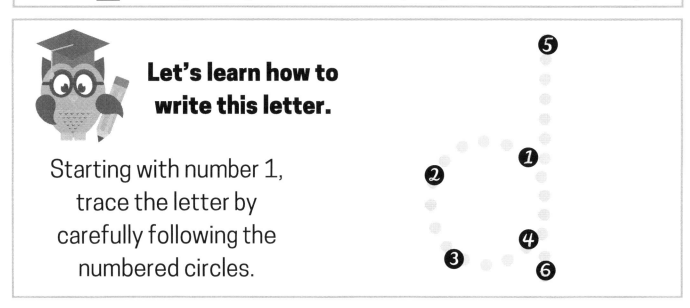

Let's learn how to write this letter.

Starting with number 1, trace the letter by carefully following the numbered circles.

Now let's practice! Trace the letters using the example above.

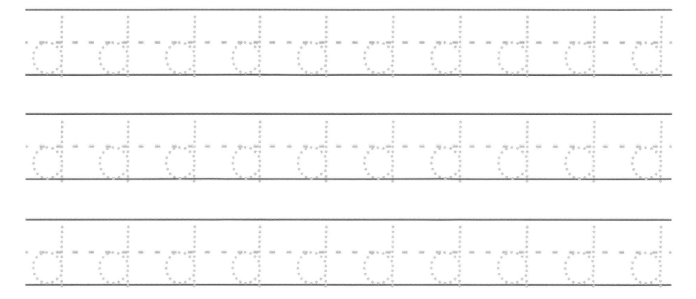

Your turn! Write the letter on your own.

d

A B C **D** E F G H I J K L M N O P Q R S T U V W X Y Z

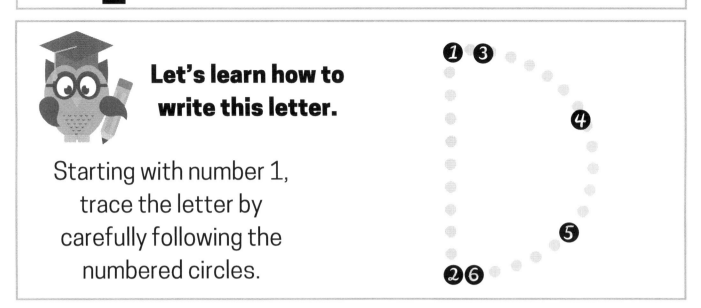

Let's learn how to write this letter.

Starting with number 1, trace the letter by carefully following the numbered circles.

Now let's practice! Trace the letters using the example above.

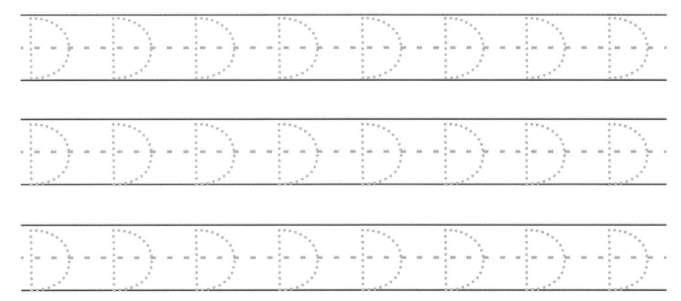

Your turn! Write the letter on your own.

D

a b c d **e** f g h i j k l m n o p q r s t u v w x y z

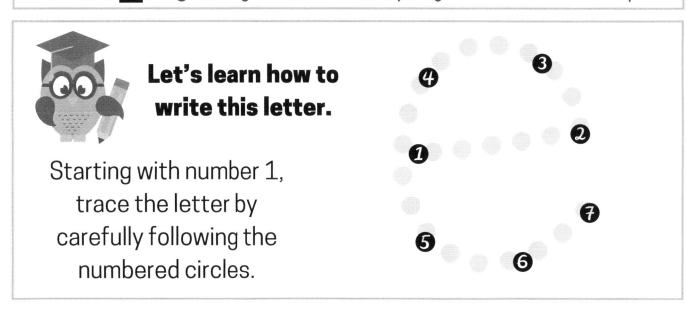

Let's learn how to write this letter.

Starting with number 1, trace the letter by carefully following the numbered circles.

Now let's practice! Trace the letters using the example above.

e e e e e e e e e e

e e e e e e e e e e

e e e e e e e e e e

Your turn! Write the letter on your own.

e

a b c d e f g h i j k l m n o p q r s t u v w x y z

A B C D **E** F G H I J K L M N O P Q R S T U V W X Y Z

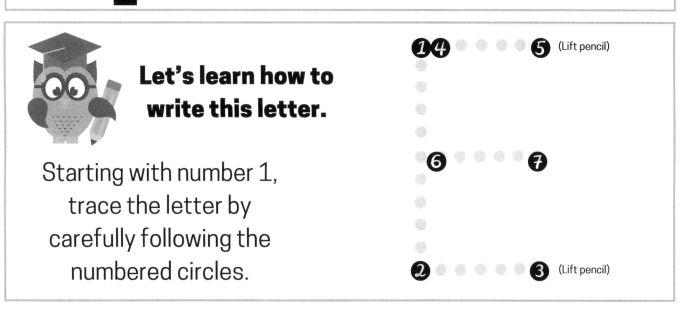

Let's learn how to write this letter.

Starting with number 1, trace the letter by carefully following the numbered circles.

1 4 • • • • **5** (Lift pencil)

6 • • • • **7**

2 • • • • **3** (Lift pencil)

Now let's practice! Trace the letters using the example above.

Your turn! Write the letter on your own.

E

a b c d e **f** g h i j k l m n o p q r s t u v w x y z

Let's learn how to write this letter.

Starting with number 1, trace the letter by carefully following the numbered circles.

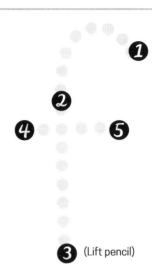

1

2

4   **5**

3 (Lift pencil)

Now let's practice! Trace the letters using the example above.

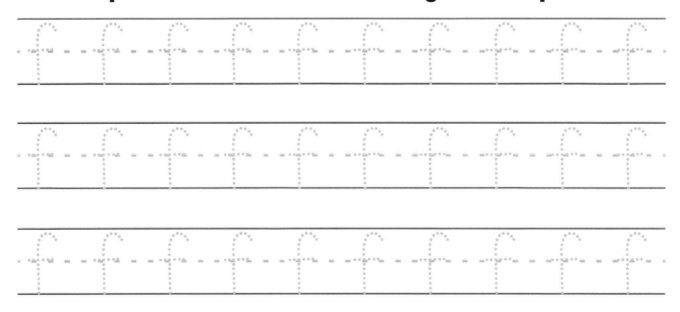

Your turn! Write the letter on your own.

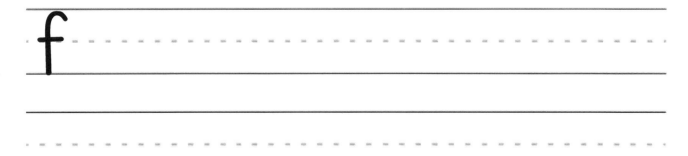

A B C D E **F** G H I J K L M N O P Q R S T U V W X Y Z

Let's learn how to write this letter.

Starting with number 1, trace the letter by carefully following the numbered circles.

① ③   ④ (Lift pencil)

⑤   ⑥

❷ (Lift pencil)

Now let's practice! Trace the letters using the example above.

Your turn! Write the letter on your own.

F

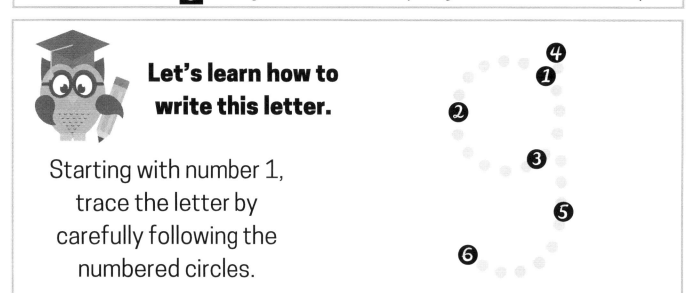

a b c d e f **g** h i j k l m n o p q r s t u v w x y z

Let's learn how to write this letter.

Starting with number 1, trace the letter by carefully following the numbered circles.

Now let's practice! Trace the letters using the example above.

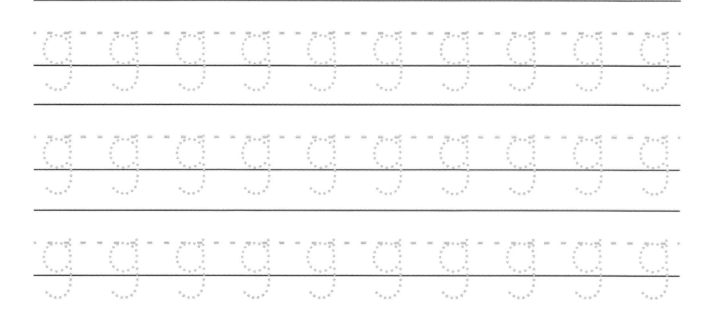

Your turn! Write the letter on your own.

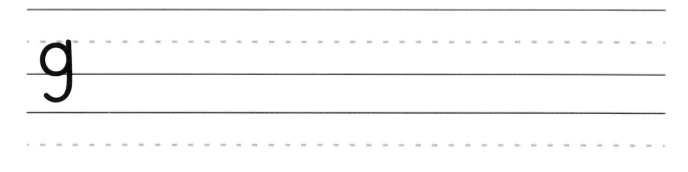

g

A B C D E F **G** H I J K L M N O P Q R S T U V W X Y Z

Let's learn how to write this letter.

Starting with number 1, trace the letter by carefully following the numbered circles.

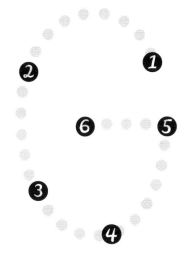

Now let's practice! Trace the letters using the example above.

G G G G G G G

G G G G G G G

G G G G G G G

Your turn! Write the letter on your own.

G

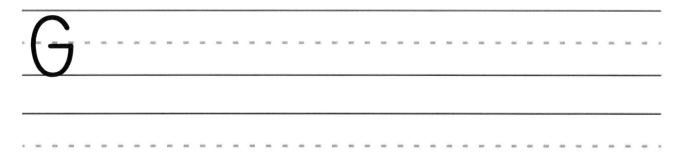

a b c d e f g **h** i j k l m n o p q r s t u v w x y z

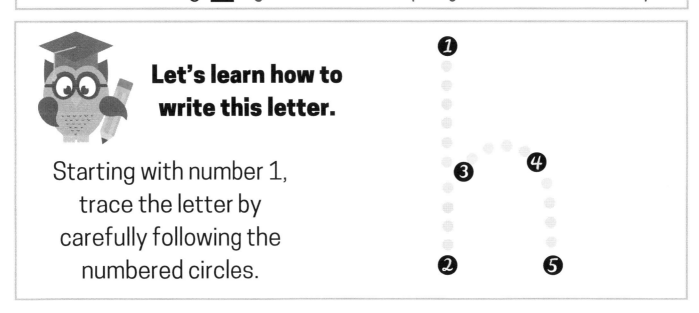

Let's learn how to write this letter.

Starting with number 1, trace the letter by carefully following the numbered circles.

❶
❸ ❹
❷ ❺

Now let's practice! Trace the letters using the example above.

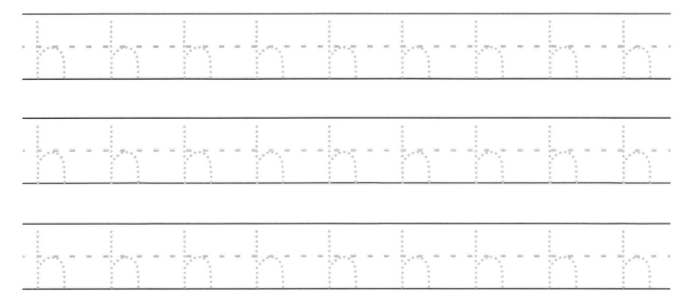

Your turn! Write the letter on your own.

h

a b c d e f g h i j k l m n o p q r s t u v w x y z

A B C D E F G **H** I J K L M N O P Q R S T U V W X Y Z

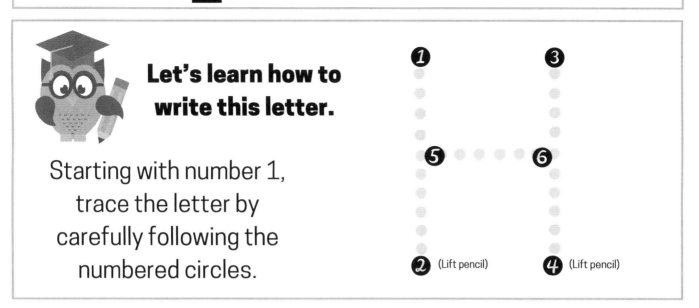

Let's learn how to write this letter.

Starting with number 1, trace the letter by carefully following the numbered circles.

① ③
⑤ ⑥
② (Lift pencil) ④ (Lift pencil)

Now let's practice! Trace the letters using the example above.

Your turn! Write the letter on your own.

H

a b c d e f g h **i** j k l m n o p q r s t u v w x y z

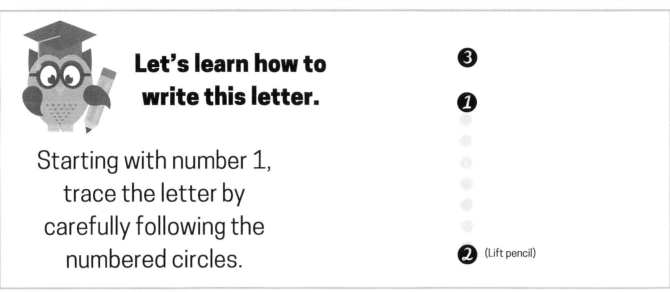

Let's learn how to write this letter.

❸

❶

❷ (Lift pencil)

Starting with number 1, trace the letter by carefully following the numbered circles.

Now let's practice! Trace the letters using the example above.

Your turn! Write the letter on your own.

i

Let's learn how to write this letter.

Starting with number 1, trace the letter by carefully following the numbered circles.

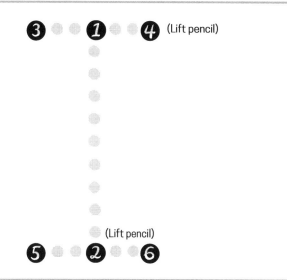

3 • • **1** • • **4** (Lift pencil)

(Lift pencil)

5 • • **2** • • **6**

Now let's practice! Trace the letters using the example above.

Your turn! Write the letter on your own.

I

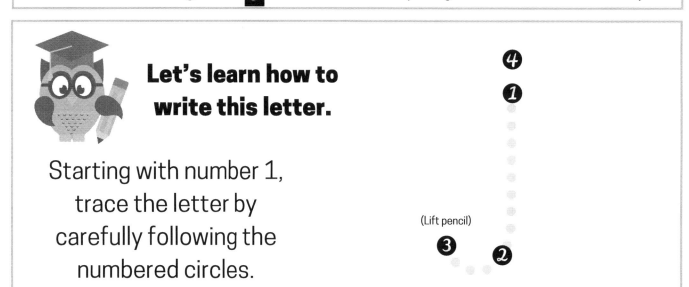

Let's learn how to write this letter.

Starting with number 1, trace the letter by carefully following the numbered circles.

(Lift pencil)

Now let's practice! Trace the letters using the example above.

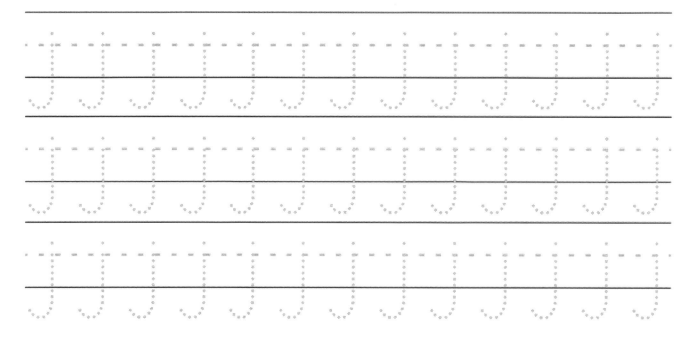

Your turn! Write the letter on your own.

j

A B C D E F G H I **J** K L M N O P Q R S T U V W X Y Z

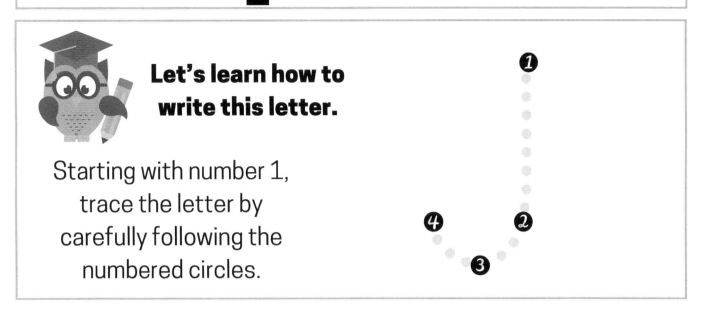

Let's learn how to write this letter.

Starting with number 1, trace the letter by carefully following the numbered circles.

Now let's practice! Trace the letters using the example above.

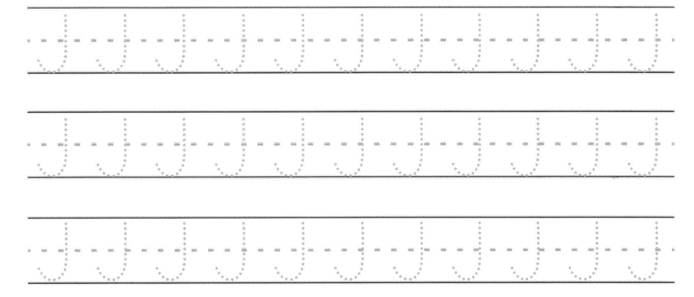

Your turn! Write the letter on your own.

J

a b c d e f g h i j **k** l m n o p q r s t u v w x y z

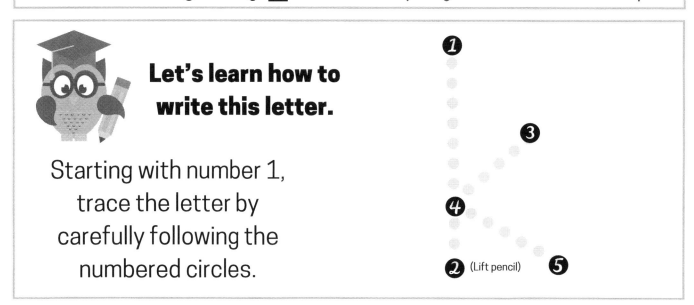

Let's learn how to write this letter.

Starting with number 1, trace the letter by carefully following the numbered circles.

❶
❸
❹
❷ (Lift pencil) ❺

Now let's practice! Trace the letters using the example above.

Your turn! Write the letter on your own.

k

A B C D E F G H I J **K** L M N O P Q R S T U V W X Y Z

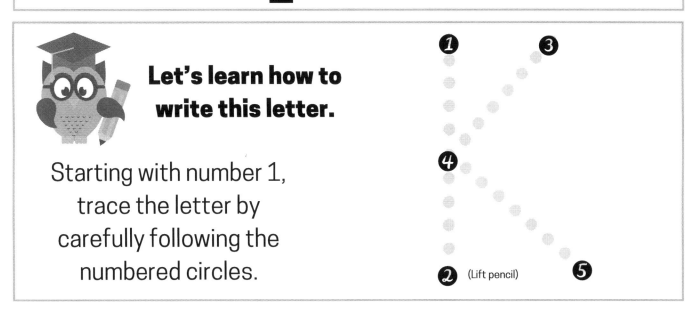

Let's learn how to write this letter.

Starting with number 1, trace the letter by carefully following the numbered circles.

(Lift pencil)

Now let's practice! Trace the letters using the example above.

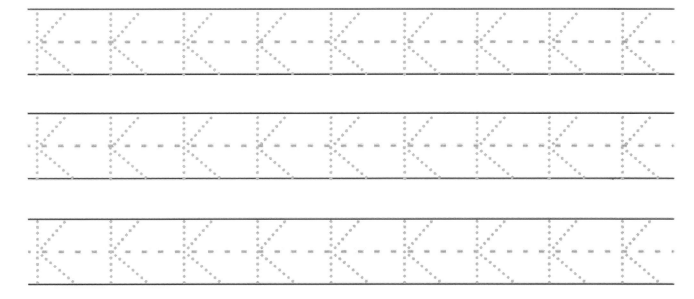

Your turn! Write the letter on your own.

K

a b c d e f g h i j k **l** m n o p q r s t u v w x y z

Let's learn how to write this letter.

❶

Starting with number 1, trace the letter by carefully following the numbered circles.

❷

Now let's practice! Trace the letters using the example above.

Your turn! Write the letter on your own.

A B C D E F G H I J K **L** M N O P Q R S T U V W X Y Z

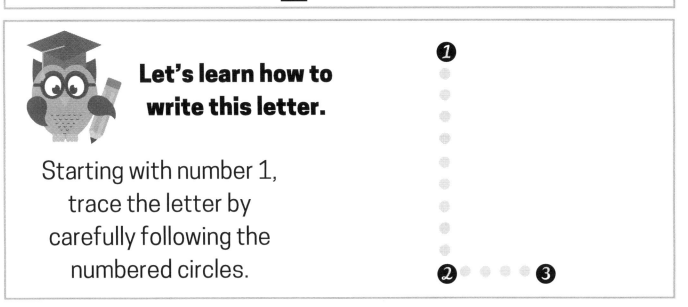

Let's learn how to write this letter.

Starting with number 1, trace the letter by carefully following the numbered circles.

Now let's practice! Trace the letters using the example above.

Your turn! Write the letter on your own.

a b c d e f g h i j k l **m** n o p q r s t u v w x y z

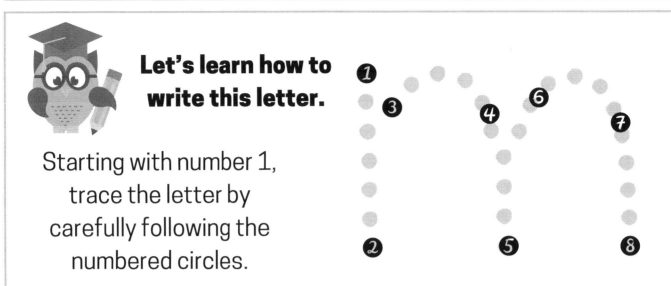

Let's learn how to write this letter.

Starting with number 1, trace the letter by carefully following the numbered circles.

Now let's practice! Trace the letters using the example above.

m m m m m m m m m m m m

m m m m m m m m m m m m

m m m m m m m m m m m m

Your turn! Write the letter on your own.

m

A B C D E F G H I J K L **M** N O P Q R S T U V W X Y Z

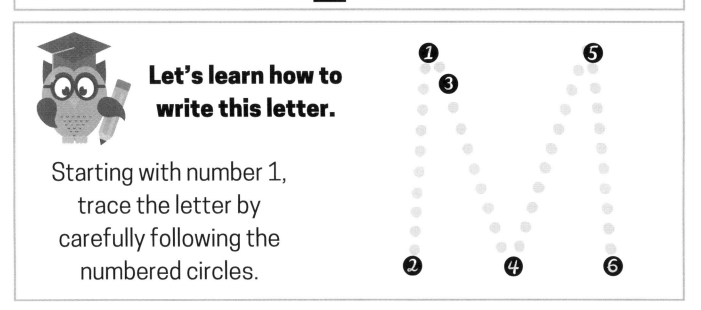

Let's learn how to write this letter.

Starting with number 1, trace the letter by carefully following the numbered circles.

Now let's practice! Trace the letters using the example above.

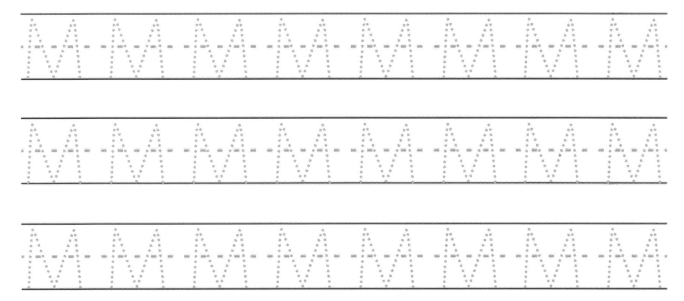

Your turn! Write the letter on your own.

M

a b c d e f g h i j k l m **n** o p q r s t u v w x y z

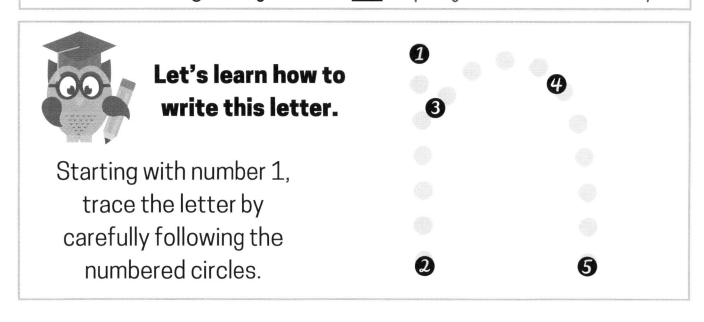

Let's learn how to write this letter.

Starting with number 1, trace the letter by carefully following the numbered circles.

❶ ❷ ❸ ❹ ❺

Now let's practice! Trace the letters using the example above.

Your turn! Write the letter on your own.

n

ABCDEFGHIJKLM**N**OPQRSTUVWXYZ

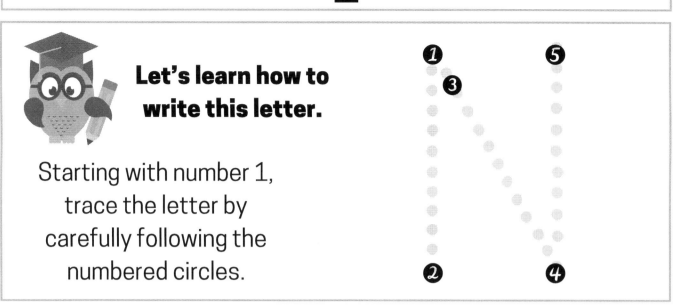

Let's learn how to write this letter.

Starting with number 1, trace the letter by carefully following the numbered circles.

Now let's practice! Trace the letters using the example above.

N N N N N N N N N N N N

N N N N N N N N N N N N

N N N N N N N N N N N N

Your turn! Write the letter on your own.

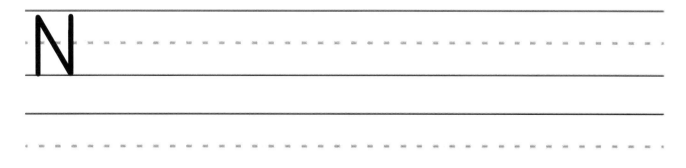

a b c d e f g h i j k l m n **o** p q r s t u v w x y z

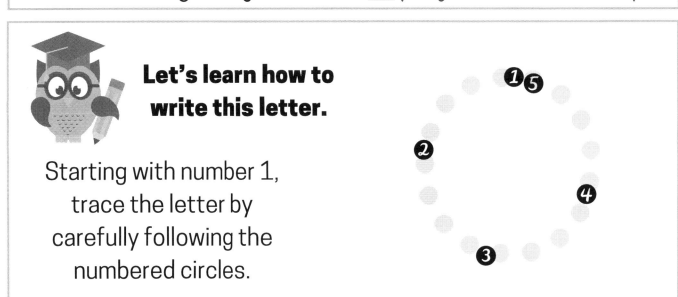

Let's learn how to write this letter.

Starting with number 1, trace the letter by carefully following the numbered circles.

Now let's practice! Trace the letters using the example above.

Your turn! Write the letter on your own.

O

A B C D E F G H I J K L M N **O** P Q R S T U V W X Y Z

Let's learn how to write this letter.

Starting with number 1, trace the letter by carefully following the numbered circles.

Now let's practice! Trace the letters using the example above.

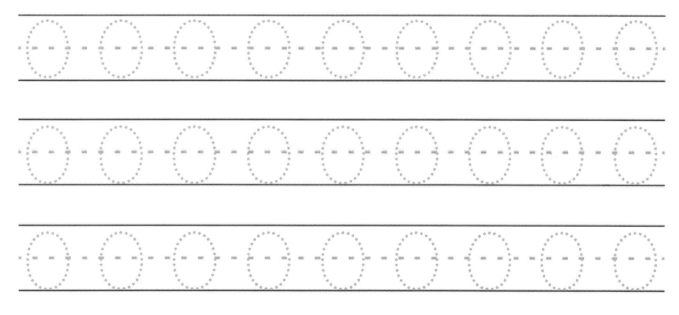

Your turn! Write the letter on your own.

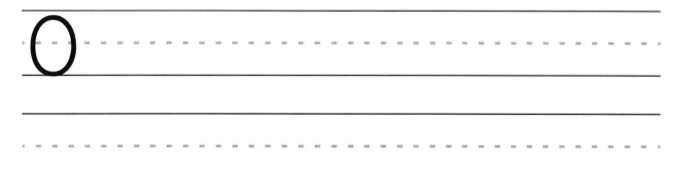

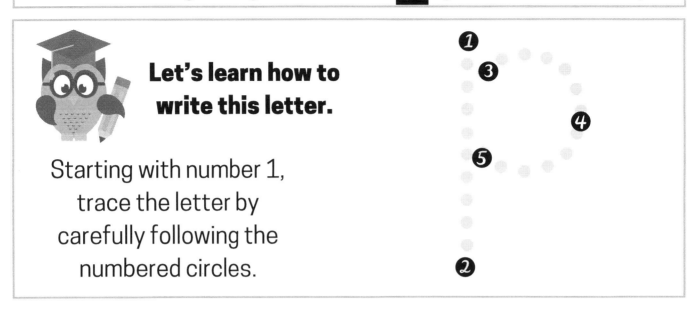

Let's learn how to write this letter.

Starting with number 1, trace the letter by carefully following the numbered circles.

Now let's practice! Trace the letters using the example above.

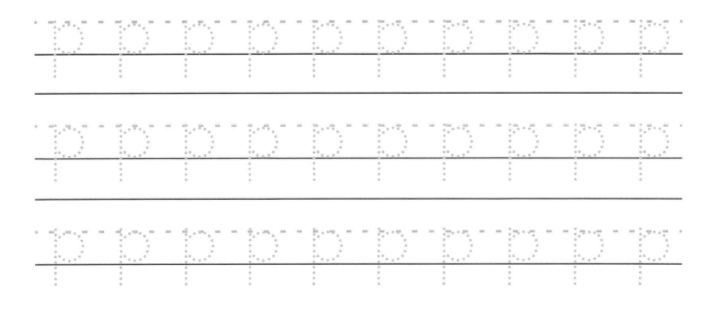

Your turn! Write the letter on your own.

p

A B C D E F G H I J K L M N O **P** Q R S T U V W X Y Z

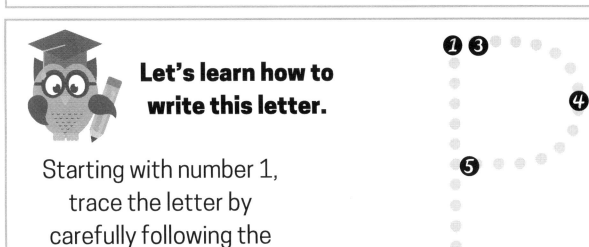

Let's learn how to write this letter.

Starting with number 1, trace the letter by carefully following the numbered circles.

Now let's practice! Trace the letters using the example above.

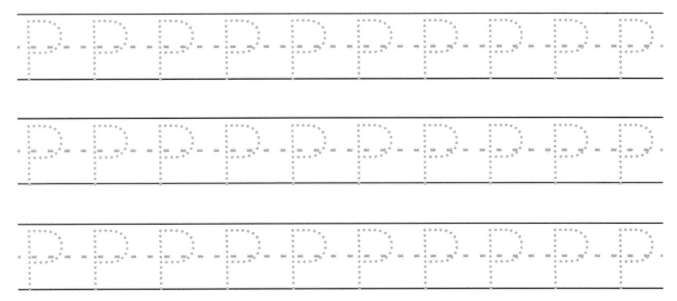

Your turn! Write the letter on your own.

P

a b c d e f g h i j k l m n o p **q** r s t u v w x y z

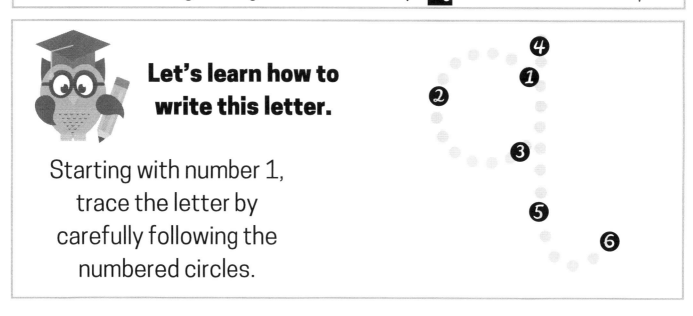

Let's learn how to write this letter.

Starting with number 1, trace the letter by carefully following the numbered circles.

Now let's practice! Trace the letters using the example above.

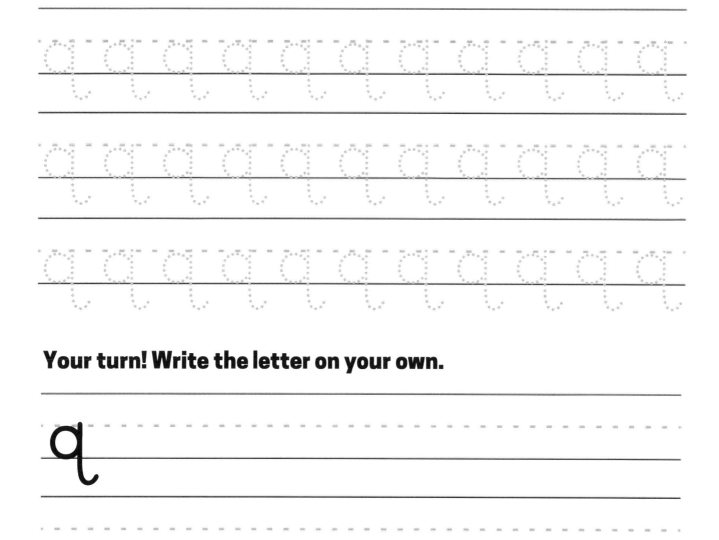

Your turn! Write the letter on your own.

q

A B C D E F G H I J K L M N O P **Q** R S T U V W X Y Z

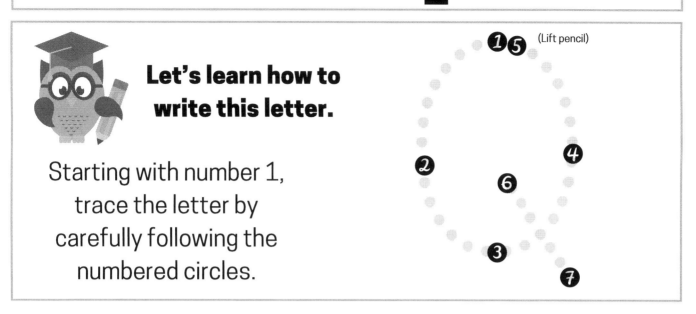

Let's learn how to write this letter.

Starting with number 1, trace the letter by carefully following the numbered circles.

(Lift pencil)

Now let's practice! Trace the letters using the example above.

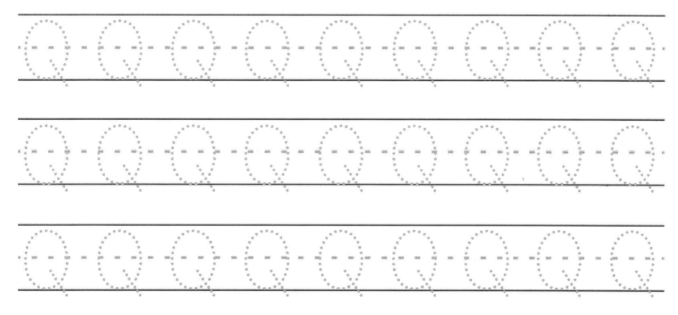

Your turn! Write the letter on your own.

Q

a b c d e f g h i j k l m n o p q **r** s t u v w x y z

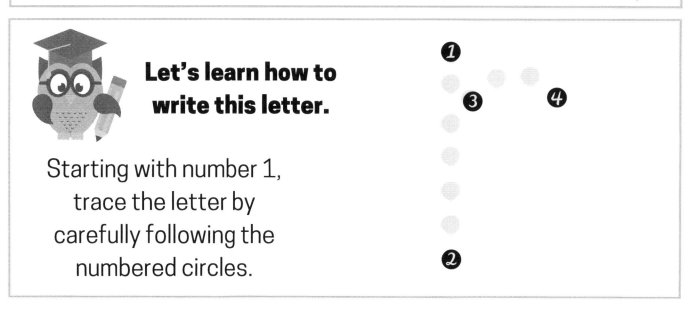

Let's learn how to write this letter.

Starting with number 1, trace the letter by carefully following the numbered circles.

❶
❸ ❹

❷

Now let's practice! Trace the letters using the example above.

Your turn! Write the letter on your own.

r

A B C D E F G H I J K L M N O P Q **R** S T U V W X Y Z

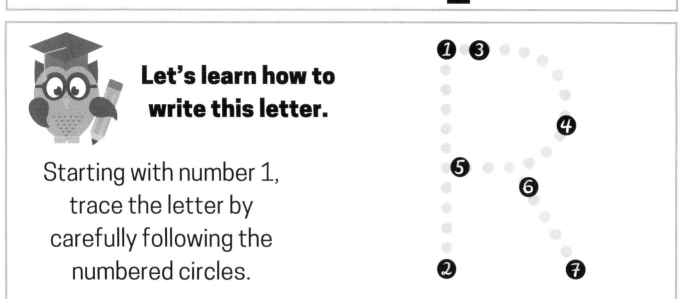

Let's learn how to write this letter.

Starting with number 1, trace the letter by carefully following the numbered circles.

Now let's practice! Trace the letters using the example above.

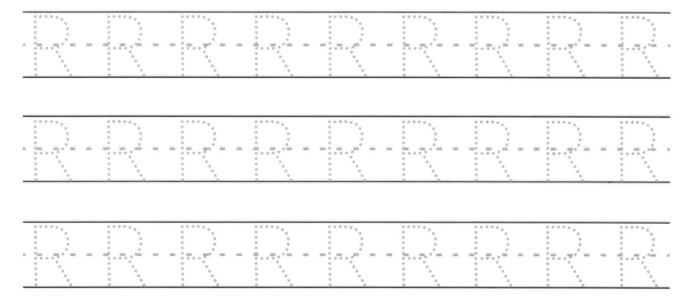

Your turn! Write the letter on your own.

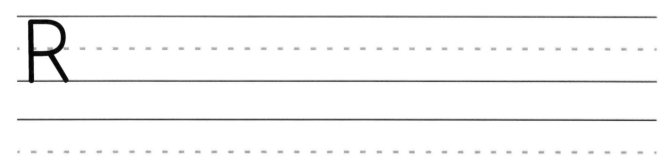

a b c d e f g h i j k l m n o p q r **s** t u v w x y z

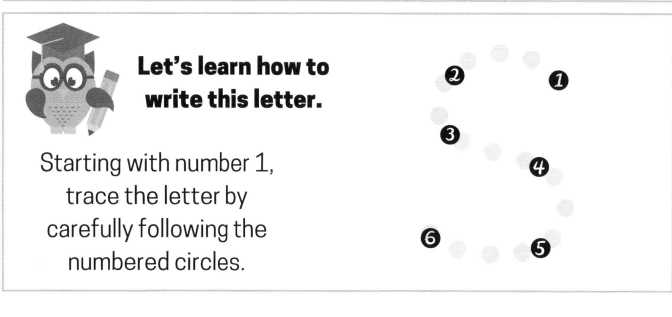

Let's learn how to write this letter.

Starting with number 1, trace the letter by carefully following the numbered circles.

Now let's practice! Trace the letters using the example above.

Your turn! Write the letter on your own.

S

A B C D E F G H I J K L M N O P Q R **S** T U V W X Y Z

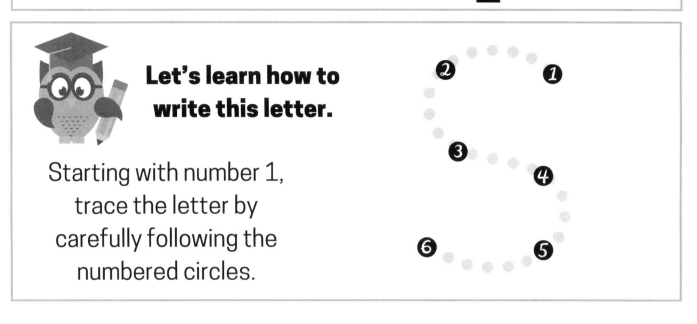

Let's learn how to write this letter.

Starting with number 1, trace the letter by carefully following the numbered circles.

Now let's practice! Trace the letters using the example above.

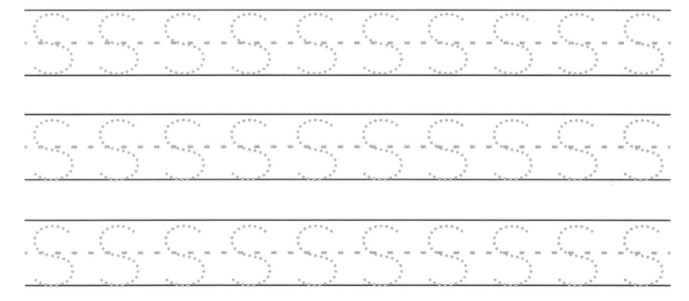

Your turn! Write the letter on your own.

S

a b c d e f g h i j k l m n o p q r s **t** u v w x y z

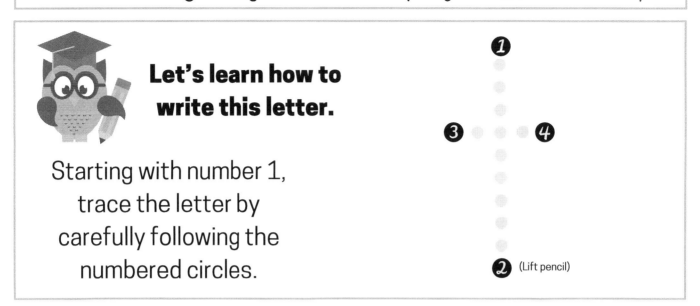

Let's learn how to write this letter.

Starting with number 1, trace the letter by carefully following the numbered circles.

❶

❸ ❹

❷ (Lift pencil)

Now let's practice! Trace the letters using the example above.

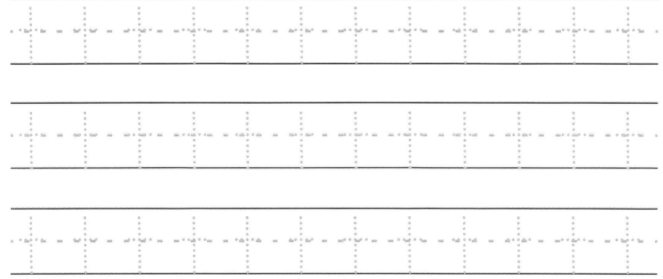

Your turn! Write the letter on your own.

A B C D E F G H I J K L M N O P Q R S **T** U V W X Y Z

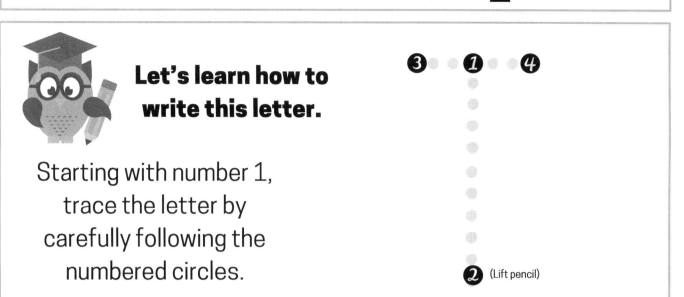

Let's learn how to write this letter.

Starting with number 1, trace the letter by carefully following the numbered circles.

❸ ❶ ❹

❷ (Lift pencil)

Now let's practice! Trace the letters using the example above.

Your turn! Write the letter on your own.

T

a b c d e f g h i j k l m n o p q r s t **u** v w x y z

Let's learn how to write this letter.

Starting with number 1, trace the letter by carefully following the numbered circles.

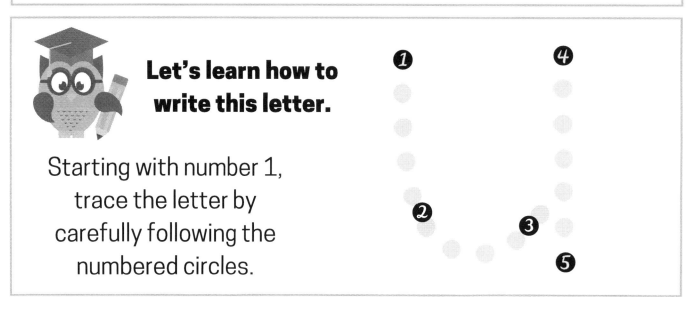

Now let's practice! Trace the letters using the example above.

Your turn! Write the letter on your own.

u

A B C D E F G H I J K L M N O P Q R S T **U** V W X Y Z

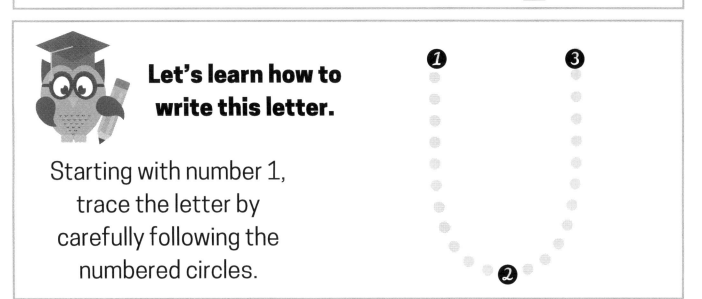

Let's learn how to write this letter.

Starting with number 1, trace the letter by carefully following the numbered circles.

Now let's practice! Trace the letters using the example above.

Your turn! Write the letter on your own.

U

a b c d e f g h i j k l m n o p q r s t u **v** w x y z

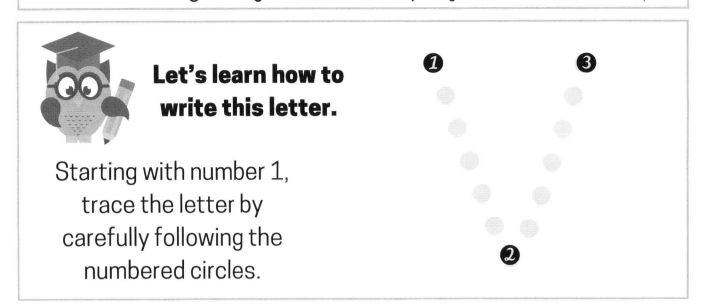

Let's learn how to write this letter.

Starting with number 1, trace the letter by carefully following the numbered circles.

Now let's practice! Trace the letters using the example above.

v v v v v v v v v v v v v v v

v v v v v v v v v v v v v v v

v v v v v v v v v v v v v v v

Your turn! Write the letter on your own.

V

A B C D E F G H I J K L M N O P Q R S T U **V** W X Y Z

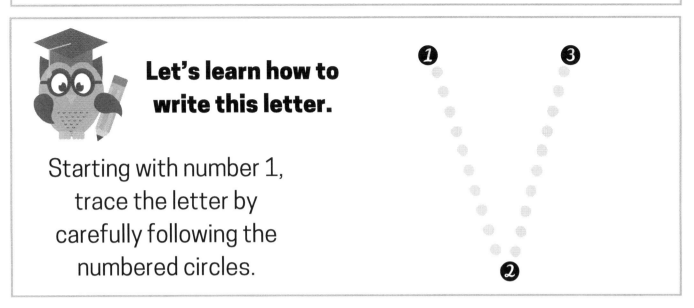

Let's learn how to write this letter.

Starting with number 1, trace the letter by carefully following the numbered circles.

Now let's practice! Trace the letters using the example above.

Your turn! Write the letter on your own.

V

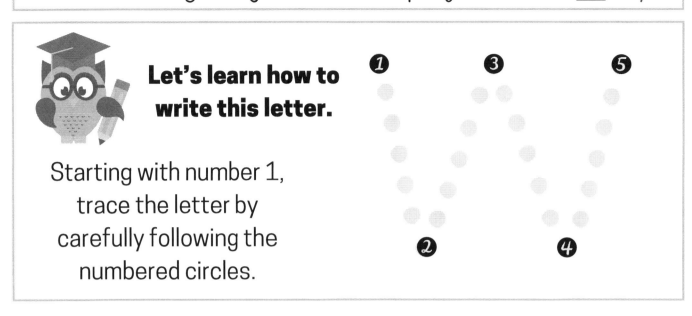

Let's learn how to write this letter.

Starting with number 1, trace the letter by carefully following the numbered circles.

Now let's practice! Trace the letters using the example above.

Your turn! Write the letter on your own.

W

A B C D E F G H I J K L M N O P Q R S T U V **W** X Y Z

Let's learn how to write this letter.

Starting with number 1, trace the letter by carefully following the numbered circles.

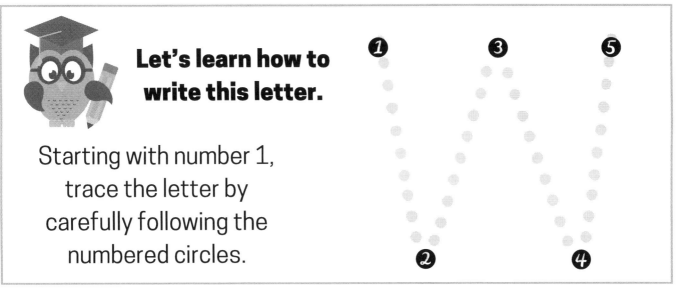

Now let's practice! Trace the letters using the example above.

Your turn! Write the letter on your own.

W

a b c d e f g h i j k l m n o p q r s t u v w **x** y z

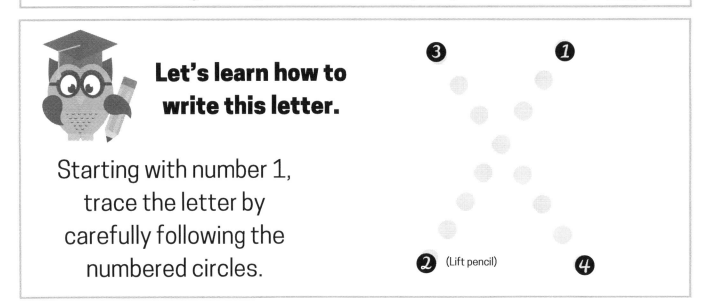

Let's learn how to write this letter.

Starting with number 1, trace the letter by carefully following the numbered circles.

3 **1**

2 (Lift pencil) **4**

Now let's practice! Trace the letters using the example above.

X X X X X X X X X X X X X X

X X X X X X X X X X X X X X

X X X X X X X X X X X X X X

Your turn! Write the letter on your own.

X

Let's learn how to write this letter.

Starting with number 1, trace the letter by carefully following the numbered circles.

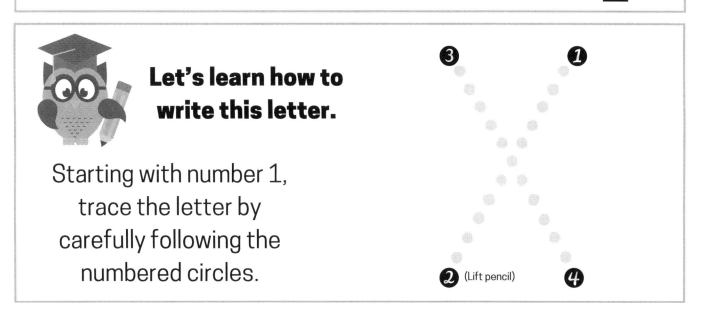

❸   ❶

❷ (Lift pencil)   ❹

Now let's practice! Trace the letters using the example above.

X X X X X X X X X

X X X X X X X X X

X X X X X X X X X

Your turn! Write the letter on your own.

X

Let's learn how to write this letter.

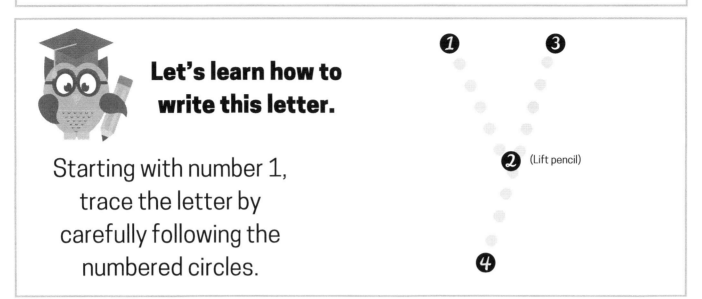

Starting with number 1, trace the letter by carefully following the numbered circles.

Now let's practice! Trace the letters using the example above.

Y Y Y Y Y Y Y Y Y Y Y Y Y Y Y Y

Y Y Y Y Y Y Y Y Y Y Y Y Y Y Y Y

Y Y Y Y Y Y Y Y Y Y Y Y Y Y Y Y

Your turn! Write the letter on your own.

y

Let's learn how to write this letter.

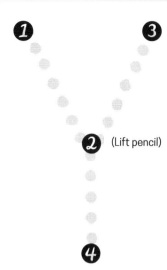

❶ ❸

❷ (Lift pencil)

❹

Starting with number 1, trace the letter by carefully following the numbered circles.

Now let's practice! Trace the letters using the example above.

Y Y Y Y Y Y Y Y Y Y Y

Y Y Y Y Y Y Y Y Y Y Y

Y Y Y Y Y Y Y Y Y Y Y

Your turn! Write the letter on your own.

Y

a b c d e f g h i j k l m n o p q r s t u v w x y z

Let's learn how to write this letter.

Starting with number 1,
trace the letter by
carefully following the
numbered circles.

❶ ❷

❸ ❹

Now let's practice! Trace the letters using the example above.

Your turn! Write the letter on your own.

z

A B C D E F G H I J K L M N O P Q R S T U V W X Y **Z**

Let's learn how to write this letter.

Starting with number 1, trace the letter by carefully following the numbered circles.

Now let's practice! Trace the letters using the example above.

Z Z Z Z Z Z Z Z

Z Z Z Z Z Z Z Z

Z Z Z Z Z Z Z Z

Your turn! Write the letter on your own.

Z

a b c d e f g h i j k l m n o p q r s t u v w x y z

A B C D E F G H I J K L M N O P Q R S T U V W X Y Z

 **Use this page to practice any letters that you found difficult.**

a b c d e f g h i j k l m n o p q r s t u v w x y z

A B C D E F G H I J K L M N O P Q R S T U V W X Y Z

 **Use this page to practice any letters that you found difficult.**

a b c d e f g h i j k l m n o p q r s t u v w x y z

A B C D E F G H I J K L M N O P Q R S T U V W X Y Z

 **Use this page to practice any letters that you found difficult.**

Part 2: Writing Words

(They start easy, but get harder!)

baby baby baby baby

Trace the word then copy it in the space beneath.

girl girl girl girl girl

glad glad glad glad

Trace the word then copy it in the space beneath.

hand hand hand

truck truck truck

Trace the word then copy it in the space beneath.

name name name

late late late late late

Trace the word then copy it in the space beneath.

wind wind wind

nice nice nice nice

Trace the word then copy it in the space beneath.

candy candy candy

lunch lunch lunch

Trace the word then copy it in the space beneath.

away away away

club club club club

Trace the word then copy it in the space beneath.

what what what

drive drive drive

Trace the word then copy it in the space beneath.

very very very very

each each each each

Trace the word then copy it in the space beneath.

tree tree tree tree

farm farm farm

Trace the word then copy it in the space beneath.

riding riding riding

cattle cattle cattle

Trace the word then copy it in the space beneath.

dinner dinner dinner

heard heard heard

Trace the word then copy it in the space beneath.

family family family

inches inches inches

Trace the word then copy it in the space beneath.

Juice   Juice   Juice

Kitten Kitten Kitten

Trace the word then copy it in the space beneath.

Large Large Large

Merry Merry Merry

Trace the word then copy it in the space beneath.

Picture Picture Picture

Shield Shield Shield

Trace the word then copy it in the space beneath.

Running Running

Under Under Under

Trace the word then copy it in the space beneath.

Value Value Value

Winter Winter Winter

Trace the word then copy it in the space beneath.

Xray Xray Xray Xray

remember remember

Trace the word then copy it in the space beneath.

yesterday yesterday

Different Different

Trace the word then copy it in the space beneath.

Suddenly Suddenly

President President

Trace the word then copy it in the space beneath.

Sentence Sentence

happiness happiness

Trace the word then copy it in the space beneath.

Beautiful Beautiful

medicine medicine

Trace the word then copy it in the space beneath.

maximum maximum

Part 3: Writing Sentences

Copy the sentence above.

If you don't get it right first time try again in the remaining space.

If you do get it right, write it again as practice.

I am going to stand next to my best friend.

She checked every store near her house for bread.

The water in the pond is two inches below the plant.

She has taken
her own lunch
from home today.

His father wants him to raise his grades in class.

We stood around a tree on the first day of school.

Do not show her the round stone that broke.

The electric current moves in waves through the wire.

He read the story under the covers with a light.

My uncle lives one hundred miles east of here.

We had to wrap John's wrist and knee after he fell.

Shall we knock on my sister's door to see how she is?

An atom is a tiny particle you cannot see using your eyes.

He will tell you something funny to make you laugh.

Watch the cloud change direction in the sky.

We have a chance to travel in a big train today.

My teacher showed me how to answer the math problem.

They were scared when the mirror crashed down.

I picked up a
blue pencil off the
table in her office.

What is the price to put a fence around this space?

We cannot get close to the huge giraffe in the zoo.

Which operation will help me solve the equation?

They had to walk through the forest in the night.

His voice makes a noise that will annoy you.

The sound from the fountain began to grow louder.

We are learning multiplication and division in class.

My father read a book by an author who taught writing.

Made in the USA
San Bernardino,
CA

56916689R00062